PUFFIN BOOKS

TRAINS, TRACKS AN

Trains are fascinating. There are many different types to look out for – passenger trains, goods trains, underground trains, steam trains, even driverless trains. A railway journey is an opportunity to see all sorts of things like bridges, tunnels, stations, signals and level crossings.

Discover here the world of trains for yourself, from the very first steam locomotives to the latest high-speed trains. With lots of interesting facts, quizzes and things to do and look for, and a chapter with practical ideas to start you train-spotting, this book is the ideal introduction to these exciting machines.

Sue Finnie has travelled extensively in Europe; she is a freelance writer and editor of educational and children's books. She is married with two sons and lives in Perthshire, Scotland.

Jim Finnie works in the leisure industry. He has been a rail enthusiast since childhood, travelling extensively in Britain and Europe to pursue his interest. He is married to Sue Finnie.

Also by Sue Finnie
Europe Up and Away!

TRAINS, TRACKS AND TRAVEL

Sue and Jim Finnie

Illustrated by
Ian Winton

PUFFIN BOOKS

THANKS

The authors would like to thank the following for their help in compiling the text and providing picture references:

Dennis Smith, Traction Yard Supervisor, BR
Mike Bowler, Public Relations Assistant, InterCity, BR
British Rail Educational Service
M. Keane, ScotRail, BR
Björn Halldén, Swedish State Railways

PUFFIN BOOKS

Published by the Penguin Group
Penguin Books Ltd, 27 Wrights Lane, London W8 5TZ, England
Penguin Books USA Inc., 375 Hudson Street, New York, New York 10014, USA
Penguin Books Australia Ltd, Ringwood, Victoria, Australia
Penguin Books Canada Ltd, 10 Alcorn Avenue, Toronto, Ontario, Canada, M4V 3B2
Penguin Books (NZ) Ltd, 182–190 Wairau Road, Auckland 10, New Zealand

Penguin Books Ltd, Registered Offices: Harmondsworth, Middlesex, England

First published 1992
10 9 8 7 6 5 4 3 2 1

Filmset in Monophoto Century Schoolbook

Printed in England by Clays Ltd, St Ives plc

Contents

Trains are amazing!
Trains can travel under the ground,
climb mountains and cross deserts.
They can hang from a rail in the sky or
float on air. There are hundreds of
different types of train.

Why we need trains

PASSENGER TRAINS

Trains which carry people are called **passenger trains**. Some people travel by train every day. Some people use the train only for special journeys.

Why do you think the people on this **platform** are waiting for the train?

- To get to school?
- To get to work?
- To go shopping?
- To visit friends or family?
- To go out for the day?
- To go on holiday?

Some people have never been on a train.

In Britain all railways are run by a large company called **British Rail** – **BR** for short. See how many different places you can spot the BR emblem (two lines and two arrowheads).

Passenger trains get very busy in the morning when everyone is trying to get to school or to work at the same time, and again in the evening when they are going home. These busy times are called the **rush hour**. The rest of the day trains are not nearly so busy.

If you travel by train for a short trip, you usually catch a small **local train** which stops at all the stations.

If you are going on a long journey, you catch an **express train** which travels fast. Express trains only stop at the biggest and most important stations. They travel on a **main line**.

What is a main line?
A railway line which links cities and towns that are a long distance apart.

GETTING ABOUT

Can you imagine what it would be like if you had to walk everywhere? Travelling would be slow ... and your feet would be sore!

Travel hasn't always been as easy as it is today.

The wheel was invented about 5,000 years ago. No one knows who the inventor was, but we can all be grateful to him or her. The wheel has been used for transport in many different ways since then. Trains are one very important way.

The wheel is thousands of years old, but

railways are much more recent – only about 160 years old. Before 1825 there were no railways as we know them today. The fastest way to travel was in a coach or wagon pulled by horses. These were slow and bumpy. In wet weather their wheels got stuck in the mud.

By 1850 there were railways all over Britain. You can read about the first railways on page 52. For the first time ever it was possible to travel as fast as 50 kilometres per hour. People and goods could be moved around much more quickly than before. And weather was not nearly so much of a problem: snow-ploughs were fixed on the front of trains to clear the tracks. This meant that trains could run even in the worst weather.

Trains took town people to the seaside and the countryside for the first time in their lives.

FREIGHT TRAINS

Trains are not just for passengers. All sorts of things are moved by trains. Oil and coal are taken to factories. Goods are carried from factories to wherever they are needed.

Trains which carry goods are called

10

freight trains. Freight trains are strong. One train can carry as much freight as 25 lorries.

Goods are loaded into containers at the factory. The containers are brought by road to the train terminal. Big cranes lift the containers on to flat wagons.

There are different types of freight wagon because some goods need special containers to carry them. Have you seen any of these?

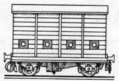

- A refrigerated van (carrying food)

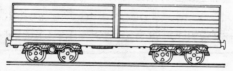

- A container wagon (carrying boxes of electrical goods, for example)

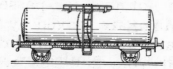

- A chemical wagon (carrying danger-ous liquids)

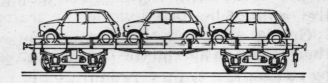

- A car transporter (carrying new cars)

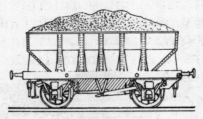

- A hopper (carrying gravel or grain)

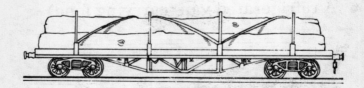

- A timber wagon (carrying wood)

MAIL TRAINS

During the night, while you are asleep, special trains called **mail trains** carry letters and parcels all over the country.

Postal workers work in special compartments on the train. Letters posted during the day can be sorted while the train is speeding along in the dark. They are ready to be delivered the next morning.

DIFFERENT WAYS TO TRAVEL

Of course, trains are not the only way to get about. How many different means of transport can you think of? The pictures will help you.

SOMETHING TO DO

Make a list of all the journeys you go on. Write down *where* you are going and *how* you travel. *Why* are you going on the journey?

How does rail travel compare with travel by plane and car?

✓ = Yes ✗ = No

Good points	Train	Plane	Car
Goes fast			
Can run even in bad weather			
You can move about inside			
There are tables so you can eat, work and play games			
Bad points			
Costs a lot of money			
Uses a lot of energy			
Can get stuck in traffic jams/sometimes arrive late			
Can be difficult to park			

Can you think of any other reasons to travel (or not to travel) by train?

Trains are a good way to travel. You can find out all about trains and railways in the following chapters. Let's start by looking at a station.

Inside a station

You get on or off a bus at a bus-stop.
You get on or off a train at a **station**.

The largest station in the world is in the USA. It is **Grand Central Station** in New York. It has 46 platforms and 67 tracks.

Stations are not all the same, though. They can be big or small. Some stations – **halts** – are not much more than a stop and are just tiny wooden or concrete platforms. Halts are found mostly in the countryside where only a few people live and there are never many passengers waiting for the train.

Most stations are not as big as Grand Central or as small as a halt. They are somewhere in between. Which is the biggest station you have been to?

DIFFERENT TYPES OF STATION

Terminus
A station at the start (or end) of a line is

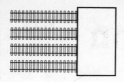

called a **terminus**. A terminus is usually a big station because several rail tracks start and finish there.

Through station

This is a station along the line. Trains come from one direction on one track, and go in the other direction on another. Some stations can be a terminus for short-trip trains as well as a through station for long-distance expresses.

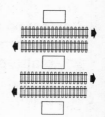

Junction station

In a **junction** station, there are lines passing through that go in more than two directions. Passengers often change trains at a junction. Some stations have the word 'junction' in their name (like Watford Junction).

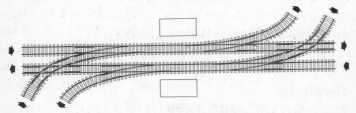

Did you know?
- There are over 2,400 stations in Britain.

- Britain's largest station is Clapham Junction in South London. It has 17 platforms.

- The longest platform in Britain is at Gloucester. It is 603 metres long.

- Beasdale Halt, on the Fort William–Mallaig line in Scotland, is just a small platform where you have to wave your arm to signal to the driver to stop the train!

- The station with the longest name is Gorsafawddachaidraigddanheddogleddollonpenrhynarevrdraethceredigion. You can see the name printed on a board 19.5 metres long if you travel on the Fairbourne Steam Railway, near Barmouth, North Wales.

- The oldest station in the world is Liverpool Road Station in Manchester.

STATION BUILDINGS

Stations are usually busy places. The bigger the station, the more there will be to see. The Grand Central in New York has 550 trains and 180,000 people passing through it each day!

Station buildings can be modern or traditional (built a long time ago).

Some old stations, like St Pancras in London and Glasgow Central, were built to look like palaces. Modern stations are not as fancy.

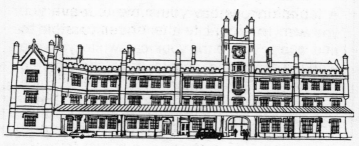

A traditional station

A modern station

Stations can be noisy places. Next time you are in a big station, stop for a minute and listen. Can you hear announcements from the loudspeakers? What other sounds can you hear?

Fifty years ago, stations were even busier than they are today. They were noisy and smoky. Nowadays stations are cleaner.

A lot of stations have their own car-parks. If you work in a big city it can be impossible to find a place to park your car while you are working, so some people drive their car to the station nearest their home and then catch a train to take them to work in the city. These people are known as **commuters**.

Big stations provide special **trolleys** to help people with heavy luggage. You put your bag on and push the trolley along yourself.

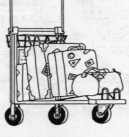

This trolley can only be used by British Rail staff. It is called a **BRUTE** (short for British Rail Universal trolley). It is blue. It carries parcels and post. There are red trolleys too. They belong to the Post Office.

Sometimes you can see an electric truck like this pulling trolleys.

SPOT IT!

Go to a station.

Use this list to check off some of the things you can see.

	Tick		Tick
Arrivals board		Journey TV screens	
Baggage truck		Leaflets	
Bridge		Litter-bin	
Café		Locomotive driver	
Cleaners		Loudspeakers	
Clock		Luggage trolley	
Departures board		Newspaper stand	
Flowers in tubs or baskets		Platform number	
Information desk		Platform ticket machine	

	Tick		Tick
Porters		Waiting-room	
Porters with red or green flags		**Others:**	
Posters			
Royal Mail Vans			
Station Manager's office			
Subway			
Taxi rank and taxis			
Ticket-collector			
Ticket machine			
Ticket-office			
Timetables			
Toilets			
Train guard			

BUYING YOUR TICKET

Everyone needs a **ticket** when they travel on a train. Your ticket proves you have paid for your trip. The longer your journey is, the more your ticket will cost. You can buy a ticket from the ticket-office or from a machine. Read more about tickets on page 33.

What ticket can you buy at a station which doesn't give you the right to travel on a train and go anywhere?

A platform ticket. In some stations, you need one if you want to go on to the platform to look at the trains or to meet someone.

TIMETABLES

Timetables tell people what time their train will leave the station and when it will arrive at its destination. They help travellers to plan their journeys, and they help the railway to schedule trains too. To keep a railway running smoothly, everything has to be well planned. There are so many trains going to all sorts of different places that it can be difficult to organize them if delays occur.

Northtown – Bigtown – Middletown – Littletown – Southtown

Mondays to Saturdays

		1	
Northtown	d	0900	–
Bigtown	d	0910	–
Middletown	d	0920	–
Littletown	d	0930	–
Southtown	a	0940	–

Notes
a Arrive
d Depart
1 Also conveys First Class accommodation.

How good are you at reading timetables? Try to answer these questions. Answers on page 91.

1. How long does the journey from Northtown to Southtown take?

2. I live in Bigtown. I want to go to Littletown. What time does the train leave Bigtown? When does it get to Littletown?

3. How long does the journey from Bigtown to Littletown take?

Timetables are usually stuck on a wall or a stand. Information about trains which will soon be *leaving* is sometimes shown on a **departures board**. Information about trains which will soon be *arriving* is shown on an **arrivals board**. Modern boards are controlled by computer and include a digital clock so travellers can see how long they have to wait for their train.

The Northtown departures board might look like this:

Departures

Time	09 : 00
Platform	3

Southtown

via Bigtown

Calling at

Middletown
Littletown

Time Now

08: 15.40

Special announcements

The Southtown arrivals board might look like this:

Arrivals		
Time due	0 9 : 4 0	Time due
Estimated arrival time	ON TIME	Estimated arrival time
Platform	1 1	Platform
Northtown		

We have had a look at where we start our journey. Now let's look inside a train.

Inside a train

The first passenger trains were very uncomfortable. They were more like stage-coaches. They had wooden seats with no cushions. Sometimes there were no seats at all! There was no heating. There were no windows, lights or springs. We are lucky that things are different today.

INTERCITY 125

The **InterCity 125** is a high-speed train (HST for short) used for journeys between cities. As its name suggests, it can travel at a top speed of 125 miles per hour (200 kilometres per hour). It is the fastest diesel train in the world. The carriages are modern and comfortable.

There are large windows so you can see a lot as you travel along. These windows do not open. This is to make sure you will be safe. The compartments are air-conditioned. That means the temperature inside the train is automatically controlled.

SOMETHING TO DO

When you are on a train, look out of the window. How many of these can you see?

Bridge	
Canal	
Church	
Cows or sheep	
Factory	
Fields	
Flowers	
Houses	
Other trains	
River	
Roads	
Sea	
Trees	

Did you notice anything else?

Long trains are made up of several **carriages** joined together. There is a **power unit** (with a driver's cab and conductor-guard's compartment) at each end. Each passenger carriage is given a letter: A, B, C, etc. You can see this letter on the outside of the carriage. A list of station stops might be on the window of the carriage door, too.

Have you ever seen a little ticket sticking out of the back of some of the seats? These are **reservation** tickets. If a train is going to be busy, people often reserve their place in advance to make sure they get a seat. The reservation slip shows the carriage number and seat number.

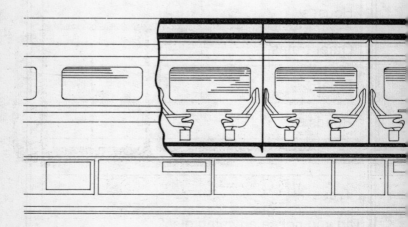

Some trains have 'wraparound' doors at the end. This gives a wide space when opened. This is helpful for wheelchairs, prams, or if you have a big suitcase to lift on to the train.

Doors inside the train are usually automatic – they open themselves if a person comes towards them. This is useful if you have your hands full carrying luggage or hot drinks.

Sometimes there is a space near the door where you can leave suitcases and big bags. Otherwise you can put your bags in the space between the seat-backs. There is a shelf above your head to put smaller bags or coats.

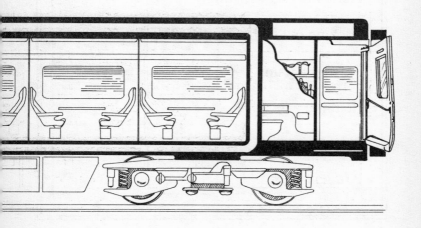

InterCity trains are equipped for long journeys. There are toilets at the end of each carriage and usually a **buffet car** or **dining-car** where you can get something to eat or drink.

Passengers spend their time on journeys in different ways.

SOMETHING TO DO	
Next time you are on a train, see how many people are:	
Chatting	
Having a snack	
Listening to a Walkman	
Looking out of the window	
Playing a game	
Reading	
Sleeping	
Writing	

TICKETS

On the train, the conductor-guard comes round to check the tickets. He will probably print a number on your ticket with a special machine. This is to show that he has seen it, and so that it can't be used again. If you want another ride, you'll have to buy another ticket!

Most tickets are **standard class**. But you can buy a **first-class** ticket. It is more expensive and allows you to travel in a first-class carriage, which is more comfortable, and usually less crowded.

> Choose a *single* ticket if you only want to travel one way. If you want to go *and* come back, choose a *return* ticket.

Commuters buy **season tickets**. These last for a week, a month, three months, six months or a year. This saves them having to stop to buy a ticket every day, and it's cheaper, too!

You may have seen some people using **railcards**. These make train travel cheaper. They are to encourage special groups of people to use the train a lot: families, students and old people, for example.

All tickets cost money. Why does the railway need the money from tickets? How is your fare money spent?

Paying wages to drivers, conductor-guards, station staff, track workmen and office workers

Mending tracks, bridges, stations, and equipment

Repairing and cleaning locomotives and **rolling-stock** (coaches, trucks and wagons)

Buying new locomotives and rolling-stock (which cost a lot of money!)

Buying electricity and diesel oil to make loco-motives go

Keeping stations tidy

Improving safety

Making the rail system more modern (buying computers and other new machines)

STICKERS AND SIGNS

On first-class carriages you may see a sticker like this:

Another sticker you might see on the train window is this:

This means no smoking is allowed in that carriage.

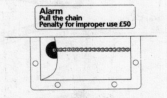

Have you ever seen a sign like this near a lever or a cord? Pulling the lever or cord attracts the driver's attention and stops the train if there is an emergency.

PEOPLE WHO WORK ON TRAINS
Ticket examiner

Driver   Conductor-guard

37

INSIDE THE DRIVER'S CAB

Driving a train is an important job. The train driver is responsible for the safety of all the passengers. Inside the cab there is a large windscreen with wipers to give a clear view of the track ahead.

Drivers sit on the left of the cab on all trains. Some newer trains are 'driver-only'. This means there is no conductor-guard. The driver presses a button to close automatic doors from his cab.

Here is a picture of the controls in an HST cab:

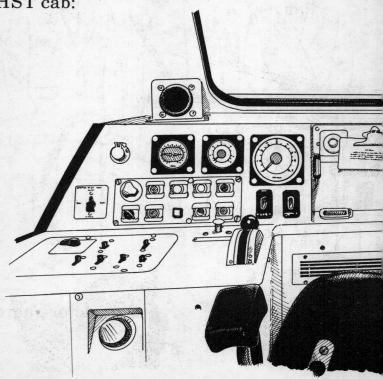

INSIDE THE CONDUCTOR-GUARD'S VAN

The conductor-guard keeps a number of items in his own special compartment. They are only used if there is an emergency.

They include:

- fire extinguisher
- emergency coupling
- ladder to help people off the train
- rail clips for changing signals to 'danger'

SOMETHING TO DO

Keep a record of your journeys.
Here's what to do:

1. Get an exercise book or scrap book.
2. Write out the following information each time you travel by train:

> **Date:**
> From: (*name of station*)
> To: (*name of station*)
> Reason for journey:
> Train departed at: (*time*)
> Train arrived at: (*time*)
> (Look at a timetable. Did your train leave and arrive on time?)
> Number of stops:
> Name of train (if there is one):
> Ticket number:
> Coach number:
> Seat number:

3. Copy this map of Britain and draw in your route.
4. Draw or write in anything interesting you notice on your trip.

Along the track

CUTTINGS AND EMBANKMENTS

When railways were being built in the nineteenth century, the first step was to make the land ready. Railways could not go up or down steep hills. So early railway companies had to dig or blast their way through hills, to form what we call **cuttings**.

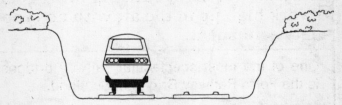

Where the land level dropped sharply, a different plan was needed. **Embankments** were built.

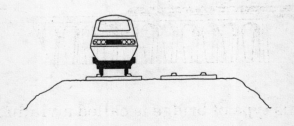

TUNNELS AND BRIDGES

Have you been through any **tunnels**?
Have you been across any railway
bridges?

Where hills are too steep, valleys too
deep and rivers too wide, tunnels and
bridges have been built. Many of these
bridges and tunnels are very long. They
were difficult to design and dangerous
to build. In early tunnels, men worked
by candle-light. Sometimes the tunnels
collapsed. Workers building bridges had
to work high up in the air with no proper
safety equipment.

One of the most spectacular railway bridges
is the Forth Railway Bridge in Scotland.

The Channel Tunnel, between Britain and
France, is the most famous railway tunnel.

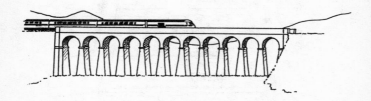

This type of bridge is called a **viaduct**.

THE TRACK

Trains travel along a track, sometimes called the **permanent way**. You can see railway tracks all over the country. There are 16,587 kilometres of track in Britain. Each track is made of two steel rails. These are joined to **sleepers** with fixing-plates or shoes. The tracks sit on a bed of **ballast**.

The distance between the two rails is

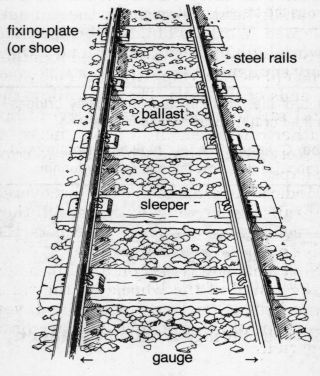

fixing-plate (or shoe) →

steel rails

ballast

sleeper

← gauge →

known as the **gauge**. In Europe and the USA the gauge is always the same: 1.43 metres.

What is a sleeper?
A block of wood or concrete. Sleepers keep rails the same width apart.

What is ballast?
Little rocks which help rain-water to drain away. Ballast also cushions the track and stops the trains vibrating.

On older lines, rails were joined together by fish-plates leaving little gaps between the ends of the rails. The gaps allow the metal rail to expand (get bigger) in hot weather. The coach wheels make a 'trickety-trock' sound when they go over the gaps.

Modern engineers have discovered that rails can be welded together. If they are securely bolted to heavy sleepers, the rails do not move in hot weather.

Next time you travel on a train, listen to the sound of the wheels on the rails. If you hear a 'trickety-trock' sound, you are on an old line. If not, you are on a modern line.

LEVEL CROSSINGS

Level crossings make it possible for a railway to go across a road, on the same level, so that a bridge or tunnel doesn't have to be built.

Old level crossings have big, heavy swing-gates which stop cars from crossing the rails if a train is coming.

Modern level crossings are barriers which move up and down. They come down automatically when a train is

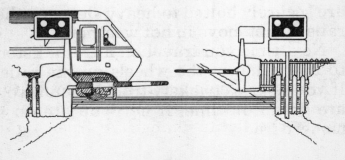

coming. Red lights flash and a bell rings.
Why do you think this is?

SIGNALS

You don't often hear of two trains crash-
ing. This is largely thanks to **signals**.
Signals are vital to safety on a railway,
especially on busy stretches of rail with
lots of fast trains rushing from place to
place.

Signals tell the driver whether the
track ahead is clear. Signals are a bit
like traffic-lights on roads.

There are two main types of signal in
Britain. Old signals are like big arms.
They are called semaphore signals. The
position of the arm tells the train driver
whether it is safe to drive on.

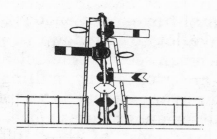

Modern signals are run by electricity.
When a train goes past a signal, it
makes the lights change. A green light

changes to red after a train has passed by the signal.

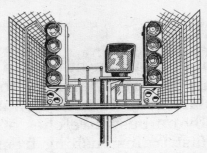

For safety, these signals are linked to the driver's cab, inside the train.

On an electric signal, there are different coloured lights. The lights tell the train driver whether to stop, go or move forward carefully.

SIGNAL-BOXES AND CONTROL CENTRES

Old **signal-boxes** are made of wood. They have lots of windows so that the signalmen can see the track clearly. The signals are worked by pulling levers. These levers are attached to wires which make the semaphore arms move.

Nowadays most of these old signal boxes have been replaced. Instead we have signal **control centres**. Inside a modern control centre, big rail maps are

worked by computers. Different coloured lights show the positions of all the signals, points and trains. The rail staff can control the signal lights at the touch of a button.

POINTS

Points are movable rails. They are used to divert locomotives from one track to another or on to sidings. This is necessary if tracks are being mended, if other trains break down or if there is an accident. Points are operated from the control centres.

Trains have to slow down when they come to points. They can't travel quickly over them.

Sometimes in cold weather points freeze. Then they can't move. This causes delays and doesn't make passengers very happy! Many points now have their own built-in heaters to stop this happening.

SIDINGS

When coaches, trucks and locomotives are not being used, they are often kept in marshalling yards or in **sidings** like these.

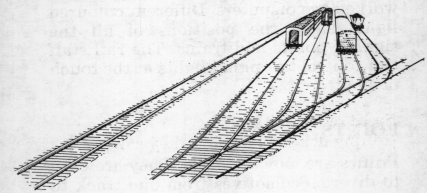

Along the track, you might also spot:

Mile markers
(giving distance to next large station)

Gradient signs

(showing how steeply a stretch of line slopes). Look at the number. After travelling that number of feet the line has sloped down ONE foot. The smaller the number, the steeper the slope.

Speed restriction signs

(telling drivers how fast they can go)

In the next chapter, find out how trains began.

The first trains

Britain was the first country in the world to build railways between towns. Before then, tracks with rails were used mostly at coal-mines. Coal from the mine was loaded on to wagons and the wagons were pulled along the track by horses.

The idea of building an engine to pull wagons along rails was exciting. It was an idea which was going to change the world.

American Indians used to call the train the 'Iron Horse'. Can you think why?

What is a locomotive?
An engine that pulls wagons or coaches along rails.

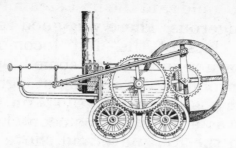

The first **locomotive** was driven by steam. It was invented in the early nineteenth century. Some people were excited. They were keen to build railways. The new locomotives could be used to link towns and cities all over the country.

Other people thought the new trains were just a silly idea that would never catch on. In the early days, lots of farmers would not let railways cross their fields.

People had been experimenting by trying to build machines using steam power for many years. There are records showing experiments done by a man called Hero of Alexandria more than 2,000 years ago.

In 1825 the first public steam railway opened. It ran between the towns of Stockton and Darlington, in the north of England.

Some people said the first steam trains were dangerous. There was good reason for this: lots of the first locomotives broke down regularly and some blew up. But the problems were soon put right.

Looking after a large steam locomotive was a dirty job. Someone had to stand on the **footplate** and shovel coal into the furnace. They were soon very hot and dirty!

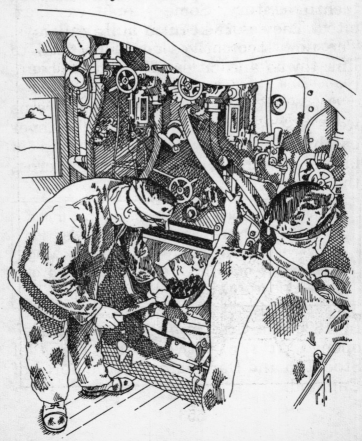

The first trains on the Stockton–Darlington line did not carry passengers, just goods.

STEPHENSON'S ROCKET

This is probably the most famous steam-engine in the whole world. It is called **The Rocket** and it was built by the English engineer **George Stephenson** in 1829. It was the first steam locomotive to pull a train between cities.

You can see **The Rocket** in the Science Museum in London. It's old and rusty today. You can get a better idea of what it used to look like if you go to York. There is a working replica of **The Rocket** outside the National Railway Museum there.

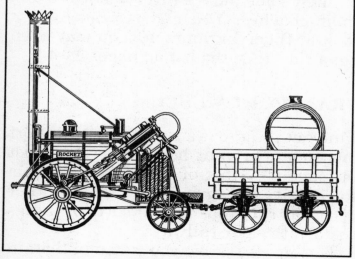

Before long, railways were built right across Britain, and in lots of other countries too. Railways were popular. Before aeroplanes and motorways, railways were by far the quickest way of travelling.

By the 1950s steam trains were replaced by diesel or electric trains. These were cleaner and faster. You can still find working steam trains in some countries. They are used in parts of India, Pakistan and China.

In Britain steam locomotives are not used on regular British Rail services any more. That doesn't mean you can't see a steam train working in Britain though. Private railways have repaired and repainted some old steam locomotives and their coaches. You can go and have a look at them for yourself. You may even get a ride! (See the list on pages 93–4.)

TRANSPORT MUSEUMS

Find out if there is a railway or transport museum near your home. There is a list on page 92. Most of them have a steam locomotive on show. You can see other types of train too, and all sorts of things to do with early railways.

The biggest railway museum in Britain

is the **National Railway Museum** at York.

GOING FASTER

As time passes, people make better and faster trains. How fast do you think trains will be able to travel in 50 years' time?

Now you know how trains became popular. But do you know how trains work? Find out in the next chapter.

How a train works

All trains need power to make the locomotive's wheels go round. There are different types of power to make a train work.

Steam trains are fuelled by coal.

Diesel trains use diesel oil.

Electric trains are powered by electricity.

Before looking at these different types of train, we need to look at the rails they travel on. The rails are like a road. But trains don't have steering wheels like cars. Trains go where the rails go.

Trains have special wheels which keep them on the rails. The main part of the wheel sits on the rail. The wheels have a wider plate on the inside called a **phlange**.

The phlange stops the train slipping off the rail and guides the wheel along. All locomotive, coach and truck wheels have phlanges.

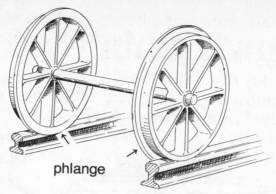

phlange

What makes the wheels of a diesel or electric locomotive go round? Look at this picture:

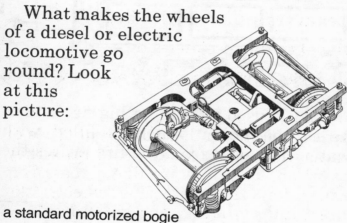

a standard motorized bogie

Inside the **bogie** is a motor which turns the wheels.

STEAM TRAINS

Steam trains are probably the most exciting of all locomotives to see and hear. They are very noisy. Locomotives are all different shapes and sizes. The *Thomas the Tank Engine* books show several different types.

A lot of coal is needed to make steam locomotives work. This coal has to be carried in a **tender** which is attached to the locomotive.

Coal is used to make a big fire underneath the boiler which is filled with water. The heat from the fire makes the

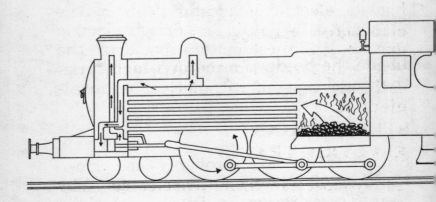

water boil. Just like a kettle, the boiling water gives off steam. This steam is forced into pressure boxes. This pressure is used to power the pistons. The big wheels of the locomotive are made to turn by rods connected to the pistons.

DIESEL TRAINS

Diesel trains took over from steam trains. People liked them better because they were quieter and stronger than steam trains.

Diesel locomotives don't need a fire or steam to make them work. They use a fuel called diesel oil. This is also the fuel used by lorries and buses, and some cars.

In these locomotives, the diesel engine has an electric generator. This makes electricity which can drive electric motors. It is these motors that drive the wheels of the locomotive. We sometimes call this type of locomotive a **diesel-electric**.

ELECTRIC TRAINS

Today most new trains are electric. Why are they popular?

There are lots of reasons:

- they can stop and start easily
- they are cheap to run
- they are clean
- they are fast and strong
- they don't make too much noise

Electric locomotives have two ways of getting electricity to work their motors. The fastest electric locomotives take power from overhead cables called **catenary**. Have a look above a railway track. You can see these cables in more and more parts of Britain.

The locomotives have bits sticking from the top of a driving coach. These bits are called **pantographs**. They pick up the electricity from the power lines and take it on board to drive the wheels.

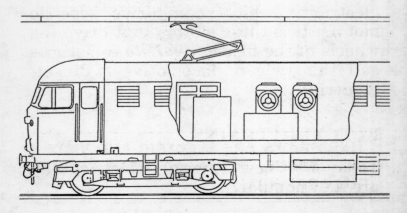

The other way of taking electricity on board is from a **third rail** on the ground. This is an electric rail which supplies electricity to trains by means of **pick-ups**. These pick-ups come out of the bottom of the train. If you have ever seen trains at Victoria or Waterloo Stations, you will know that these are driven by third-rail electricity.

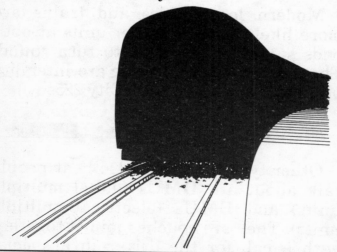

CHANGING DIRECTION

Steam trains often needed to turn round at the end of a journey. **Turntables** helped them to do this.

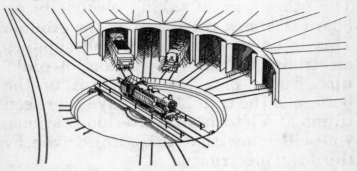

Modern locomotives and trains are more likely to have power units at both ends so they don't need to turn round. The most common of these are InterCity 125s (see page 28) or InterCity 225s.

Other types you may also hear people talk about are **DMUs** (diesel multiple units) and **EMUs** (electrical multiple units). They are coaches joined together with a cab for the driver in a special coach at each end.

Have you heard of a **push-pull train**? Perhaps you can guess how it works. It

is a train that can be pulled by a locomotive in one direction, and to save turning the train round, it can be pushed in
the other direction.

COACHES

Coaches and trucks have to be joined
firmly together and to the locomotive.
This is done by strong **couplings**. These
are linked like a short but very strong
chain.

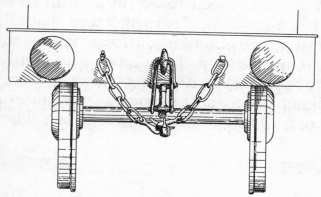

Power is taken from the locomotive –
along pipes and cables – to the coaches.
This power works the heating, air-
conditioning and lights.

Now you know how a train works, you
are ready to go and look more closely at
trains. You can be a train-spotter!

Let's go train-spotting

Lots of boys and girls – and even grown-ups – like to go train-spotting. If you go on a train journey, or see a station platform from a road, you can often see train-spotters standing in the station.

You don't need to go on a train to be a train-spotter. Train-spotters usually stand at the end of a platform, where the locomotives stop. They have a pen and a notebook and write things down.

Some train-spotters speak into cassette recorders about what they can see. They

listen to the cassette and write out all the details when they get home.

If you would like to go train-spotting you *must* remember that railways can be dangerous.

Keep to these simple rules:

- If you are at a station, **stand well back from the edge of the plat-form.**
- If you are spotting from beside the rail-way, **always keep behind the fence.**
- If you are on a train, **never put your head out of a window.**
- **Do not climb on bridges.** If you can't see over, look for a better spot some-where else.
- **Always stand well clear of electric cables or rails.**

British Transport Police
Everybody knows how important road safety is. Rail safety is just as important. Two thousand transport police-officers make sure railway passengers and staff travel in safety. They help look after railway property. As part of their job, the police-officers visit schools and brownie and cub packs to tell girls and boys about rail safety.

WHAT IS TRAIN-SPOTTING?

Every locomotive has a number, just like a motor car. Carriages and trucks have numbers too. You can see the locomotive's number on its side, on or behind the driver's cab. There are usually five figures. Each figure tells you something.

For example:

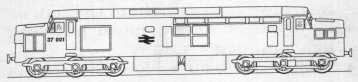

The first figure is
usually the *type*.

▼

37 001

▲   ▲

The first two figures
together are the
class.

The last three
figures tell you
which locomotive
of a particular
class it is.

68

So Number 37001 is a Type 3, Class 37, and it was the very first of its class!

It is becoming quite common for locomotives to have names as well as numbers. Electric locomotive 86213 is called *Lancashire Witch*. Diesel locomotive 47712 is called *Lady Diana Spencer*. Looking for names makes spotting easier and more fun.

There are many different ways of train-spotting.

- Stuart writes down the numbers.

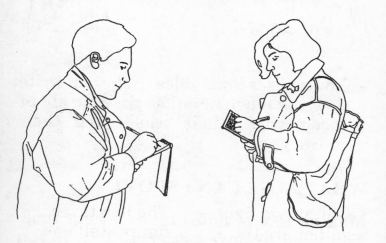

- Emily has bought a train-spotter's guide with her pocket money. It is full of information about different loco-motives. In her guide, Emily ticks off numbers as she spots the locomotives.

- Kevin writes down dates, locations, times and where the train comes from, as well as the numbers.

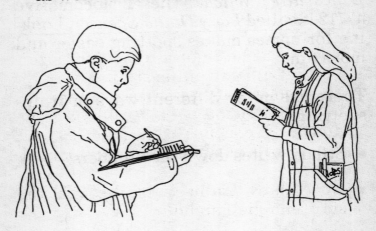

- Louise uses timetables so she can write down as much detail as possible about locomotives, their trains and their journeys.

WHAT ELSE CAN I SPOT?

Making lots of notes takes a long time. You need to have patience. But, if you are interested, there are plenty of things to look out for.

1. At the station

- Are all the locomotives the same colour?

> The colour a locomotive is painted is called its **livery**. Read more about liveries on page 74.

- Are all the locomotives the same size?
- Do they all stop at the station?
- Are some trains faster than others?
- Do the locomotives all pull the same number of coaches or trucks?
- Where are most of the trains travelling to?
- How many trains pass through the station in half an hour?

If you are standing on the platform, you might hear announcements which will help you find out how far a train is going. If you have a good map with you, you can see how far away the different destinations are. Some locomotives travel over 1,600 kilometres in 24 hours!

- Are all the coaches the same?
- Are they painted the same colour?
- Are the seats arranged differently?

Look out for special coaches:

- sleepers, which have beds in them
- mail coaches
- guards' coaches
- maintenance coaches, for repair work
- buffet cars
- Pullman coaches (dining-cars)

Coaches have information painted on either end. This tells you:

- how fast it can be pulled
- its weight
- its size
- when it was built
- when it was last painted
- how it is heated

You can also spot information about the station itself.

- How many platforms are there?
- Are they all the same length?

Use the checklist on page 22 to see what else you can spot.

2. On the train

Look back at page 40. Keeping a record of a train journey is a good way to start train-spotting.

Before you get on the train, look at the locomotive number and see if it has a name. Count the coaches. See which coach you are on.

- Are all the coaches the same?
- How many seats are in the coach?

Sometimes the conductor-guard gives information about the journey through a train speaker system.

- Can you see a ticket examiner?
- Can you see any other railway staff working on the train?

When you stop at a station, look out of your window. You might see other locomotives. Can you see if they have names?

You might pass a **depot**. A depot is where locomotives are kept when they are not in use. You might see a works depot. This is where locomotives are

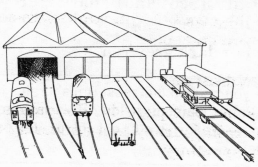

repaired. Look out too for sheds where locomotives and coaches are washed and cleaned out.

LIVERIES

Liveries make locomotives look different. Liveries can tell you where a locomotive comes from or if it is used for a special job.

Here are a few liveries to look out for:

Railfreight (goods trains) = grey with red buffers

InterCity (express trains) = dark grey/red stripe/light grey

Network SouthEast (London and south-east of England) = blue/white/red/grey

ScotRail (Scotland) = dark grey/blue stripe/light grey

Parcels = dark grey/red

Have you noticed that most British trains have their fronts painted yellow? This is a safety measure. Yellow is a bright colour. It is easily seen.

RAIL RIDERS' CLUB

How can you get to know other junior train-spotters? Why not join BR's **Rail Riders' Club**? It's for boys and girls who are interested in trains and railways. Membership (in 1992) costs £5 and you get a folder with a handbook, badge, stickers and free travel vouchers. Throughout the year you'll be sent copies of *Express*, the Rail Riders' own magazine.

If you are between 5 and 15 and would like to join, write to:

Rail Riders' Club
PO Box 20
Wetherby
LS23 6YY

Special trains

UNDERGROUND TRAINS

In big cities the roads are crowded with cars, buses and lorries. There is no space to build a local railway. So some cities have railways under the ground. They are built inside tunnels. Some are just below the surface, others are much deeper.

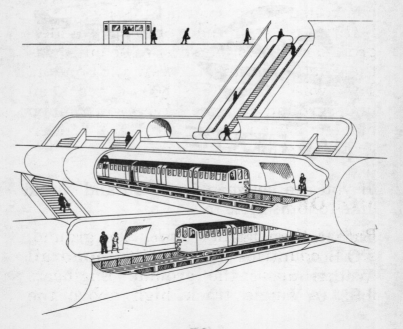

The London Underground is sometimes called the 'Tube'. Can you guess why?

At the underground station you reach the platform by going down (there are stairs, an escalator or a lift).

Often you can get around more quickly under the ground than above it. There is no traffic to slow you down. It is not often that a train breaks down and gets stuck in a tunnel, but it can happen.

Today's underground trains have electric driving coaches. They are usually controlled by a computer.

Cities all over the world have underground railways. The first to be built was the Metropolitan Railway in London. This was opened in 1863. Since then underground systems have grown much bigger. Today there are 272 Underground stations in London alone.

MONORAIL

Rather than tunnel *under* the ground, some countries have built **monorail** systems *above* the ground. Engineers build a single track high above the

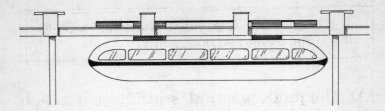

streets and buildings. On some systems the trains run on top of the rail and on others they hang down underneath it. Monorail trains are powered by electric (or diesel) motors.

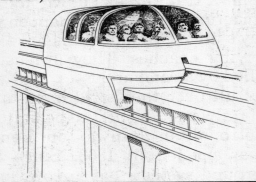

Monorail systems are popular in countries like France, Germany and Japan.

NARROW GAUGE

You may have seen very small trains running on a very narrow track. Usually these are specially built railways in parks. Some of the trains are models of steam trains.

MOUNTAIN RAILWAYS

Most trains cannot go up steep hills. This is a problem in mountain areas. So special trains have been built called **rack trains**. To stop the wheels from slipping backwards on the rails, there is a **cog-wheel** in the middle. The cog-wheel grips on to a row of teeth on a special track.

79

Another type of railway found in the mountains is the **cable railway**. A carriage is attached to a very strong cable. An engine at the top of the mountain pulls the cable and moves the carriage up the track.

SLEEPER TRAINS

Did you know that some trains have tiny bedrooms with bunk-beds? On long journeys, you can go to sleep on the train. You travel through the night and

wake up the next morning at your destination. The beds are comfortable but it can be rather noisy.

A berth in a sleeper train costs more than a seat, but it's a good way to pass a long journey.

PULLMAN TRAINS

British Rail InterCity are putting on more and more Pullman services. Perhaps you have seen a Pullman train. It is a train made up of nothing but first-class dining coaches. Business people can have their breakfast or dinner on their way to or from meetings in different parts of the country.

MOTORAIL

What do you do if you want to take your car on holiday but you don't want the long drive to get there? Easy – take your car on the train with you!

Motorail trains are special trains to carry cars and passengers. Drive your car on to the train and then go and relax in a passenger carriage. When you arrive at your destination, collect your car and drive off.

DOUBLE-DECKERS

In some countries these trains are used on busy routes. They can carry twice as many passengers as an ordinary train.

OBSERVATION CARS

Railways run through some of the most beautiful parts of the world. In Canada you can ride right through the giant Rocky Mountains. And to help you to get a really good view, there are special trains built with an observation car. This coach has huge windows all round – even in the roof – so that passengers don't miss anything.

FUN FOR KIDS

Here's an idea BR could copy!

In Sweden most inter-city trains have a carriage made into a play centre for children. You can move around, play with toys, read a book or listen to a cassette. And there's no extra cost.

TRAINS UNDER THE SEA

For more than 100 years engineers have been planning to build a tunnel under the sea between Britain and France.

Work wasn't started until 1974. The Eurotunnel Company decided the best system would be to use twin tunnels. Each tunnel contains a railway track and is about 50 kilometres long.

The **Channel Tunnel** makes travel to and from the rest of Europe much faster. Bad weather can stop ferries and hovercraft crossing the Channel. Bad weather is not a problem for trains using the tunnel. This means there is no delay in services.

You can visit the Eurotunnel exhibition centre and find out all about the tunnel.

Eurotunnel Exhibition Centre
St Martin's Plain
Cheriton High Street
Folkestone
Kent
CT19 4QD

RECORD BREAKERS

Choose the right answers to these questions. Check on page 91 to see if you are right.

Quiz

1. Do you know which is the longest railway in the world?

(a) The Trans-Siberian Railway
(b) The Stockton–Darlington Railway
(c) The Trans-Australian Railway

2. Which is said to be the most luxurious European train?

(a) The *Flying Scotsman*
(b) The *Orient Express*
(c) The TGV

3. Which is the fastest train in the world?

(a) The British InterCity 125
(b) The Russian Aurora
(c) The French TGV

4. Which country has the fastest regular train service?

(a) USA
(b) France
(c) Japan

5. Where are the longest trains in the world?

(a) Australia
(b) India
(c) Canada

Looking ahead

Are cars and buses – and aeroplanes – taking passengers away from trains? How can railways get more people to travel by train?

If more people went by train instead of by car, there would be less traffic on the roads and less pollution. Less energy would be used too.

SOMETHING TO DO

How would you make the rail system better?

Rewrite this list to show what *you* think would help most (the best idea first):

- higher speeds
- cheaper fares
- fewer delays
- more trains
- more stations
- more comfortable carriages
- more things to do on the train

Trains need to be cheap. And railways need to provide a better service if they want to get more customers. Railways are changing all the time. BR spends a lot of money on modernization. But is it enough? Britain has spent less money on its railways in recent years than most other countries.

New stations are being built but, in country areas, lots of stations have been closed down. People prefer to use their cars. On some routes the trains are almost empty. It is expensive to keep lines open if not enough people use them.

People often moan about trains being late but, in fact, about 88 per cent of all trains run on time.

LOOK ... NO DRIVER!

Running a railway is a complicated job. Computers help. They make rail travel faster, safer and cheaper.

In Lille, in France, there is an underground railway with no driver or guard. It is the first system to be worked completely automatically. The ticket machines and turnstiles are automatic too.

Perhaps in 20 years time all our stations and trains will be run by computers!

ELECTRA POWER

The new 'Electra' **InterCity 225** is the most powerful locomotive ever to run in Britain. Can you guess why it is called the '225'? It's because it has a top speed of 225 kilometres per hour.

'225' facts	
225	= top speed (kilometres per hour)
6,300	= horsepower
30	= per cent more power than similar sized electric motors
400,000	= number of kilometres it can travel in one year
576	= seats per train
4	= hours for journey from London to Edinburgh

EXPRESS – THE 158

Here is another new train to look out for – **Express**. These trains are being used on more and more medium-distance express routes. They are the latest in DMUs (diesel multiple units) and are very strong. They can travel at speeds of up to 140 kilometres per hour.

THE FLOATING TRAIN

You may be looking at the train of the future! It is a new train ... which floats! Look at the picture. How does it stay in

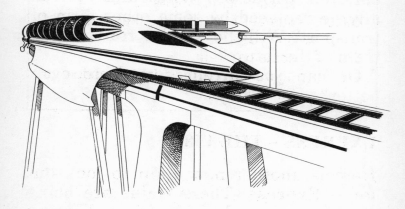

the air? There are no wheels. It is kept up in the air by electromagnetic force.

This amazing train is called the **Maglev** (<u>mag</u>netic <u>lev</u>itation). Maglev trains run on a special concrete track with magnets in it. The magnets keep the train just above the track, not touching it. They also drive it along. The journey is smooth and quiet . . . and there is no pollution.

Want to see one?
Maglev trains are often found at airports. There is one linking Birmingham airport with the National Exhibition Centre.

Will there still be trains for *your* grandchildren to ride on? Will trains eventually be replaced by some other form of transport? Will the Maglev train be the train of the future?

Or can *you* invent something even better?

Timetables, page 25:

1. 40 minutes
2. 9.10 (or ten past nine)
   9.30 (or half past nine)
3. 20 minutes

Record breakers, page 85:

1. (a) The Trans-Siberian Railway is the longest railway in the world. It stretches for 9,000 kilometres from Moscow to the Pacific Ocean. Even on a fast train, the journey takes five days!

2. (b) The *Orient Express* is probably the most luxurious European train. It has been the star of several books and films. There are thick carpets and beautiful furniture. The dining-car is like a posh restaurant. You can even take a shower on the train if you like!

3. (c) The French TGV is the fastest train in the world. In May 1990 it broke the speed record by going faster than 500 kilometres per hour. But for regular journeys it travels at a slower, safer speed.

4. (c) Japan operates the fastest regular train service in the world. The Japanese high speed train is called The Bullet. This is a good name to describe its speed and its shape.

5. (a) Australia has the longest trains in the world. They are not passenger trains. They are freight trains used to transport iron ore. A train can have more than 200 wagons. To move such an enormous weight, there are three locomotives at the front and two at the back!

Some rail and transport museums

Birmingham Railway Museum
Steam Depot, Warwick Road, Tyseley,
Birmingham

Conwy Valley Railway Museum
Betws-y-coed, Gwynedd, Wales

Darlington Railway Centre and Museum
North Road Station, Darlington, DL3 6ST

Great Western Railway Museum
Faringdon Road, Swindon, SN1 5BJ

Museum of Transport
25 Albert Drive, Glasgow, Scotland

National Railway Museum
Leeman Road, York, YO2 4XJ

Science Museum
Exhibition Road, South Kensington, London
SW7

Transport Museum
Witham Street, Belfast, N. Ireland

Some private railways

Bluebell Railway
Sheffield Park Station, nr Uckfield, E. Sussex

Bo'ness and Kinneil Railway
Bo'ness, West Lothian, Scotland

Brecon Mountain Railway
Pont Station, Dowlais, Merthyr Tydfil,
Mid Glamorgan, Wales

Dart Valley Railway
Buckfastleigh, Devon

Didcot Railway Centre
Didcot, Oxfordshire

Dinting Railway Centre
Glossop, Derbyshire

Ffestiniog Railway
Porthmadog, Gwynedd, Wales

Great Central Station
Loughborough, Leicestershire

Kent and East Sussex Railway
Tenterden, Kent

Nene Valley Railway
Wansford Station, Stibbington,
Northamptonshire

Norchard Steam Centre
New Mills, Lydney, Gloucestershire

North Norfolk Railway
Sheringham, Norfolk

North Yorkshire Moors Railway
Pickering, North Yorkshire

Railway Preservation Society of Ireland
Excursion Station, Whitehead, Co Antrim,
N. Ireland

Ravenglass and Eskdale Railway
Ravenglass, Cumbria

**Romney, Hythe and Dymchurch Light
Railway**
New Romney, Kent

Severn Valley Railway
Bridgnorth, Shropshire

Snowdon Mountain Railway
Llanberis, nr Caernarfon, Gwynedd, Wales

Strathspey Railway
Boat of Garten, Inverness-shire, Scotland

Talyllyn Railway
Tywyn, Gwynedd, Wales

West Somerset Railway
Minehead, Somerset

Index

PUFFI

APRIL
HOB LAN

Gail and her friends at Hob Lane School are back in this
sequel to *Pancake Pickle at Hob Lane*. The friends play a
daring April Fool trick on their headteacher, Gail,
Sheree and Kimbo try out some weird and wonderful
ideas in order to call up the fairies, and Gareth takes
swimming lessons – with a mermaid!

Author and journalist for many years, Robert Leeson has
published more than forty books for young people, from
school stories to fantasy and adventure. In 1985 he
received the Eleanor Farjeon Award for services to
children's literature, for encouraging pupils in reading
and creative writing in over 600 schools and for raising
funds to help equip libraries and schools in the Third
World.

By the same author

NEVER KISS FROGS
PANCAKE PICKLE AT HOB LANE

ROBERT LEESON

April Fool at
Hob Lane School

Illustrated by
Caroline Crossland

PUFFIN BOOKS

For Andreas

PUFFIN BOOKS

Published by the Penguin Group
Penguin Books Ltd, 27 Wrights Lane, London W8 5TZ, England
Penguin Books USA Inc., 375 Hudson Street, New York, New York 10014, USA
Penguin Books Australia Ltd, Ringwood, Victoria, Australia
Penguin Books Canada Ltd, 10 Alcorn Avenue, Toronto, Ontario, Canada M4V 3B2
Penguin Books (NZ) Ltd, 182–190 Wairau Road, Auckland 10, New Zealand

Penguin Books Ltd, Registered Offices: Harmondsworth, Middlesex, England

First published by Hamish Hamilton Ltd 1992
Published in Puffin Books 1993
1 3 5 7 9 10 8 6 4 2

Text copyright © Robert Leeson, 1992
Illustrations copyright © Caroline Crossland, 1992
All rights reserved

The moral right of the author has been asserted

Printed in England by Clays Ltd, St Ives plc
Filmset in Baskerville

Noddy Day

Chapter 1

"GAIL, GAIL, GET up, love!"

Gail heard her mother call, turned over and burrowed back under the bedclothes. Bed was always most comfortable in the morning. Her mother tried again. This time, her voice sounded excited.

"Gail, quick, quick!"

"Whaa-at?" Gail answered grumpily.

"Get up or you'll miss it."

"Miss what?"

1

"What's going on in the garden."

Gail struggled up and stumbled to the window. Looking out with bleary eyes, she could see nothing different. Turning she marched to the door and out on to the landing. Mum stood at the foot of the stairs, grinning. Now Gail was angry.

"What's happening in the garden? I can't see . . ."

"Grass is growing, that's what."

Then Gail remembered. It was Noddy Day again. April the First and she'd been caught.

"That wasn't fair," she yelled down the stairs. "I wasn't really awake."

There was a chuckle from the kitchen.

"Well, it got you up, any road."

When Gail got to Hob Lane corner on her way to school she was ready for

anything. She had several April Fool jokes worked out. Not new ones. She didn't think there were any. As she passed Ali's sweet shop, Sheree came out and waved.

Gail hesitated. Was it fair to try one on Sheree? Her family hadn't been here all that long. Probably she wasn't used to Noddy Day. Generously she decided to pass up this chance . . .

Sheree fell into step with her, looked sideways and said, "Your shoelace is undone."

"Pull the other," responded Gail tartly. What a little madam Sheree was. Not as innocent as she looked.

Sheree nudged her gently. "Your shoelace, love."

"Give over." Gail pushed her and marched on. Then she tripped and stumbled. She looked down. It *was*

4

undone. Sheree shook her head.

"I told you, didn't I?"

Gail made a face at Sheree. "I thought you were trying to April Fool me."

"April Fool?" Then Sheree gasped. "I'd no idea. Oh Gail." She put her hand to her mouth, then both of them burst out laughing and ran along the pavement to catch up with the rest of the gang.

It was Noddy Day all right and it
was in full swing. Gareth caught out
Kimbo. That was a giggle. He pulled
on her sleeve and held out a ball of
mixed brightly-coloured wool.

"It's been coming off your jumper
Kimbo, all down the road. I wound it
up so you could knit it back on."

Kimbo's mouth fell open. She was
always so fussy about her clothes.

Zipping open her jacket she stared,
then turned and shrieked at Gareth.

"You little . . . I've not got my
jumper on. Oh you . . ."

"Noddy, Noddy," chuckled Gareth
and sped past them.

Now they caught up with Boxer and
Grunter wrestling across the
pavement. Grunter was spluttering
with rage and beating Boxer's head

with his fist, while Boxer was helpless with laughter.

"What happened?" the others demanded.

Boxer choked. "I gave him a bit of wood in a Gorilla Gunge wrapper and he tried to bite a lump out of it. He nearly did it, too."

This tribute to Grunter's well-known appetite put him back in a good humour. By the time they reached the zebra crossing near the school gates, the six were laughing and shoving one another in high spirits.

"Jenny, Jenny!" they shouted to Jenny Wrottle, the dinner lady who doubled as crossing warden. "Jenny, your lollipop's upside down."

Jenny turned her head with its yellow hair and sunburnt face under the old leather cap and fixed them

8

with a quick, blue eye.

"Oh ah. And I'm the Queen Mother."

"Aah," they answered. "Can't catch you, Jenny."

"Right, and nor could two hundred others who tried it before you did."

They rushed round the school building into their own corner of the yard outside Class Four. Sam Bates, the caretaker, was sweeping out.

"Mr Bates!" shouted Grunter. "The

Head wants you, right away."

Sam Bates' face, fierce red under his white hair, glared at Grunter.

"I know. I've been. You know what she told me?"

Grunter stared, uncertain. "What?"

"She said, 'Give Pottsy one on the bum with your broom handle.'"

Shrieking with laughter, the six tumbled into the classroom. It was nearly full, but Miss hadn't arrived yet.

"Shall us put something on the board before she gets here?" asked Kimbo.

"You'll have to be quick," said a familiar voice behind them. Their teacher, face flushed with hurrying, hair over her eyes, marched in.

"Sit down, all of you. I've something important to say."

"Ah, come on Miss," said Boxer. "We all know it's Noddy Day."

"Right," said Miss, pulling out the register. "Are we all here?" When the names were called and ticked off, she looked up at them.

"This is important. You all know what day it is. Now that's up to noon only. So no tricks after twelve o'clock."

They nodded. Everybody knew Noddy Day tricks only worked till twelve, then the joke was on you if you tried.

Grunter put up his hand. "After that it's legging over time, Miss."

"No, it is *not*. That is what I am telling you. No legging over. No tripping up. No nothing."

"Ah, why not?" the boys protested.

"The Head has decided, for a good reason. Last year Tommy Burns was tripped up on the bank, fell and cut his head open."

The class was silent. But Grunter grumbled.

"But there's always legging over on Noddy Day."

"Not this year."

"But that's when we all get us own back."

Miss shook her head.

"That's how the big ones get their own back. What about the smaller ones?"

She fixed the class with her "listen to me" look.

"April the First you know is celebrated all over the world. In India they have Holi — when they play jokes on each other but only until one o'clock.

"It's a very old custom. It goes back

at least to Roman times. It was always
a time when ordinary people could get
a bit of their own back on those who
were powerful. The weak got even with
the strong. Not the other way round.
Right?"

That silenced everyone. The
class worked until break and then
the gang gathered on the bank at the
top of the yard. Grunter was still
complaining about legging over being
banned.

"Not fair," he said again.

"Tell you what," said Gareth, who
always thought twice as quickly as
anyone else. "If it's all about the little
people getting their own back on the
big ones, let's play an April Fool on
the Head."

"The Head?"

They all looked amazed at Gareth.

"Hey what, man?" asked Boxer.
"Gather round folks," he said. "I
have just had a brainwave."

Chapter 2

THE NEXT LESSON was creative writing. The six sent Gail to ask Miss if they could borrow the typewriter.

Miss pursed her lips. "Six of you can't all use the typewriter, Gail. What's it all for?"

"Oh, Miss, it's sort of secret. We're working on something together. You said we could make up things in groups."

"All right. But not too much noise."

That was easier said than done.

There was a bit of push and shove as they gathered round Gail. After some argument it was decided that she was best on the machine.

Boxer began. "Put at the top – 'From the Lord Mayor'."

"Get off," said Gail. "We don't have a Lord Mayor . . ."

"Right," said Gareth, "Just put 'Westchester Borough Council' at the top. Then 'Town Hall, High Street'."

"How do you spell Borough? Shall I ask Miss?"

"Nah. She'll guess we're up to something. Listen it's B-u-r-r-o-w . . ."

"Like rabbits?"

"Suppose so. Get on with it."

Gail typed the address and slid the carriage back.

She typed, "Dear Miss Carter . . ."

Kimbo said, "You are hereby

ordered to let Class Four have the afternoon off school."

"No," protested Gail. "She won't believe that."

"So what then?"

"Something like: 'The Town Council would be pleased if you would allow the school to go home after lunch today . . .'"

"Why after lunch?" asked Sheree. "Why not earlier?"

"I'm not missing my lunch," said Grunter.

"You and your stomach," snapped Kimbo.

"Shut up and get on with it," said the others.

"Tell you what," said Gareth. "Make it really good. Let's say . . . 'The Education Committee has decided . . .'"

"Yeah, loads better," they all agreed, and Gail typed while, gathered round her and leaning on one another, the others admired her work.

She finished. "Now we want a signature for the Boss."

"The Chairman," said Gareth. He leaned over and signed with a great flourish and two great lines.

"You can't read who signed it," muttered Grunter.

"Right Noddy."

The letter was folded and put in an envelope from Sheree's writing set.

"OK," she said. "What happens now?"

The rest looked at her.

"Oh no," squeaked Sheree. "Why me?"

" 'Cause you look innocent," answered Gareth. "Now listen. They won't suspect you. You're new in school. Ask Miss to let you go out — you know, then go to Mrs Hayes' office next to the Head's room. Tell her a bloke from the Council office gave it to you at the door. Just give it to her. Don't say ought else. And keep a straight face. Don't go red like."

Sheree began to blush. "I don't know if I can. Suppose she finds out?"

"Then we're all in it," said Gail.

Chapter 3

SHEREE HUNG ABOUT in the corridor outside the Head's office. The next room, where Mrs Hayes, the secretary, worked was open but quiet. She tiptoed to the door and peeped in. It was empty.

She hesitated. Then she thought, I'll just put it down and clear out. Then no one'll know who brought it. Stepping timidly forward she stood for a moment by the desk, twisting the envelope in her hands. The silence

23

around her was suddenly broken by
the old clock in the school bell tower.

Sheree jumped nervously. The old
clock banged away. "Bong, bong,
bong . . ."

Sheree giggled then stretched out
her hand with the letter.

"Sharia. What do you want, dear?"

Now her heart jumped right up into
her throat. It wasn't the secretary
who'd come in quietly behind her. It
was the Head. Sheree swung round,
pushed out her hand holding the letter,
put her head down and gabbled.

"It's from – the Town Hall . . . A
feller gave it me at the door. It's
important."

"Thank you, Sharia," the Head
sounded serious but friendly. "Did he
want a reply?"

Sheree thought she'd pass out.

Instead she dodged to one side, slipped
out of the office and without looking
back ran until she reached Class Four.

Miss looked up in surprise as she
burst in, red-faced. The six looked up
in alarm, their eyes round.

"Are you all right, Sharia?"

"Yes, thank you, Miss."
Breathlessly Sheree sat down. The
others looked sideways at her, not
daring even to whisper.

25

Chapter 4

THE LAST HALF hour to lunch dragged. The six hardly dared look up at Miss let alone at each other. Sheree, still pink with embarrassment, was almost lying on the desk trying to make herself disappear.

Then she nearly fell off her chair as the door opened and Mrs Hayes slipped in, small and grey-haired. The six felt a chill grip their stomachs. The secretary silently handed Miss a note then left.

The moments ticked by, ten minutes, twenty minutes. Then suddenly the bell went for lunch. Everybody shot up as if on springs but Miss waved them down.

"Gail, Sharia, Kimberley, Winston, Gareth and Darren, stay behind. The rest of you, off you go. And remember no legging over. Right."

The class stormed out. The six, frozen to their seats, waited.

"The Head wants to see you. Don't ask me why she asked to see all six of you. It sounds serious. I hope," she paused, head on one side, "that you haven't been up to something."

The six could not answer. Slowly, unwillingly, they shuffled out of the classroom, along to the hall and through it towards the passage where the Head's office was.

Each one tried to keep behind the
others and so they moved more and
more slowly till they had almost
stopped, when the Head's door opened
and she looked out at them.

Her face was grim. She beckoned.
"Come along. All of you."

They filed into the office and she
took her place behind her big desk and
looked them over severely. She held up
a sheet of paper. They all knew what it
was.

"Very clever," she said slowly. "I suppose you thought that because it was April the First you could get away with this."

She placed it down on the top of the desk.

"Of course, I knew who'd written it, straight away. Imagine what would have happened if I'd taken seriously this suggestion."

"Fortunately . . ." she paused.

"Fortunately, it was delivered to me just after twelve o'clock. So . . ."

Suddenly she laughed out loud.

"April noon's past and gone. You're the fools and I'm none."

Calling Up The Greenies
Chapter 1

WHEN GAIL FOUND out the secret she couldn't keep it to herself.

"You know what," she said to the others, "this is a Greenie Hill."

They were sitting on the edge of the grassy bank at the top of the school yard. Above them the trees were in full leaf, the sky was blue. The breeze was cool. But it was a great day.

The others looked baffled. Then Grunter, mouth full of pasty nicked from the kitchen, spluttered.

"Greenie? What are you on about?"

Kimbo laughed. "She means the Greenies live under here." She pointed downwards. "Don't you, Gail?"

"Right — a fairy hill."

"Ya ha!" howled Grunter, rolling over. The others grinned, embarrassed Gareth, always the gent, came to Gail's rescue.

"Belt up, gorilla gob," he said. "Why d'you reckon it's a Greenie Hill, Gail?"

She ticked off her fingers. "They're all magic trees — oak, ash and thorn."

"How d'you know?"

"I found this old book at Aunt Mandy's. It's got all about," she hesitated, "the — people in it."

She didn't say fairies for fear of setting Grunter off again. But he wasn't even listening. He'd finished his

pasty. Now he felt in his bulging jeans'
pocket and pulled out a grubby tennis
ball.

"OK fellers. Football."

He got to his feet, Boxer followed,
then more slowly Gareth. The three
girls shrugged and turned to each
other again.

Sheree was puzzled. "If it is – a
Greenie Hill – what does it mean?"

Gail thought a moment, then said,
"If we do the right thing, we might get
to see them, or hear them."

Sheree looked round at the grassy
bank and the bright green leaves
above.

"See them?" She stared. "Are you
serious?" She looked at Kimbo.
"D'you believe it?" she asked.

"Don't know." Kimbo shrugged and
said, "Don't care – much." But she

wasn't so sure. After a second she asked, "So – if we do see them – what happens then, Gail?"

"We get three wishes. If we do the right thing."

Kimbo did believe in wishes. "And this book tells you?"

"Yes. It's got all sorts in it. I can't remember everything. I just got a quick look then I had to put it back."

"Like what?"

"Well, you can only see them four times in any day. Like midnight."

Kimbo shivered. "Catch me up here at midnight."

Gail went on. "Dawn . . ."

"Worse still," put in Sheree.

"Dusk, and noon."

Kimbo looked importantly at her watch.

"Well, it's coming up for ten to

one. So we're late."

"Well," Sheree was encouraging. "It's near enough – in the hour, like. But how do we get to see them?"

Gail hesitated again. Saying the things she'd read made them sound unbelievable. "You look through a self-bored stone."

Kimbo's lip turned up. "Where'll you get one of them?"

"Don't know. But then you can stand on your head and look backwards through your legs."

"You what?"

"Like this." Gail suddenly placed her hands flat on the grass, swung up her legs and leaned back her head in one movement. Now she could see things very sharply and clearly: the stitches on Sheree's boots, the gnarled tree root, each blade of grass. And on

the blade a little globe of water
flashing green, yellow, orange in the
sun.

"Can you see anything?" demanded
Kimbo, half eager.

"Have a go yourself," gasped Gail.

Now the three of them were arched
over, feet and hands on the grass,
heads bent back. Gail could feel her
head swim. The grass circle began to
revolve slowly round her. From a great
distance she could hear faint mocking
laughter.

Suddenly into her line of sight came
an ugly face – eyes squinting, nose
turned up, tongue thrust out, lips
shaped into a grotesque pout. Then
came an ear-splitting raspberry.

"Grunter!" Gail rolled over,
bounded up and attacked him
furiously with her fists. Gareth and

Boxer stood by laughing. Sheree and
Kimbo sat, backs turned, smoothing
down their clothes and pretending
nothing had happened.

Chapter 2

NEXT DAY, GAIL tried again. As she walked to school with Sheree and Kimbo she told them what she had read in the old book at Aunt Mandy's the evening before. Once they realised what the girls were talking about, the lads walked on ahead. But at least they weren't mocking. Listening, Sheree was keen, but Kimbo doubtful.

"I'll have another go, as long as it's not doing anything stupid, like yesterday."

"Come on, Kimbo," urged Sheree, squeezing her friend's shoulder.

"No handstands, promise."

As soon as morning lessons were over, as near to noon as they could make it, the three ran up to the grass bank. The sun was high, the grass warm, the air still.

"Now what?"

"First we have to find foxglove bells, fern fronds and a four-leaved clover."

Kimbo made a face.

"They're all occard things," she grumbled.

" 'Course they are." Sheree was reproachful. "Stands to reason it can't be easy."

"Where d'we find them?"

Gail looked round the school yard. It was nearly empty. Most people had gone in to first dinner. No teacher was in sight.

"Come on, under the fence."

43

She led the way, Sheree followed,
Kimbo came third, reluctantly.

"I'm not going in the field with all
the cows, and that bull."

"They're over the other side. Miles
away. Come on."

They searched, and searched,
through the grass growing fresh and
lush, the edges of the green-covered
pond, the hedge and ditch full of
budding flowers and the quick, secret
movements of birds and little animals.

Gail felt she could spend the whole afternoon there. But the second dinner bell and hunger drove them back.

Gail met Sheree by the side of the pond. Both shook their heads.

"No foxgloves out yet."

"Lots of three-leaved clover. No four-leaf."

They climbed back through the fence to the bank where a silent Kimbo waited. She had found something. She held up a single, wilting fern leaf.

And she'd picked up something else. Around the edge of her new, white boots was a dark, brown rim. Kimbo had stepped in it. Sheree and Gail started to laugh, but stopped at the sight of her face. They went into dinner in silence.

Next day a row started on the way to school. Gail and Sheree walked

along full of plans for the next attempt
on the secrets of Greenie Hill.

"What shall we do now?" asked
Sheree. "Have you looked it up in the
book, Gail?"

"Well, there's only three more
things we can try as far as I could
make out. You wear a daisy chain,
carry a dry crust in your pocket and
wear your clothes inside out."

Sheree giggled. "How can you keep
ought in your pockets if they're inside
out?"

She turned to include Kimbo in the
conversation which was the chance *she*
was waiting for.

"Well, you count me out of the
whole stupid business. Yesterday we
nearly missed dinner and I ruined a
pair of boots."

"You never. It wiped off."

Kimbo raised her voice, glaring at Gail.

"Well, I'm fed up. Up to here. Everybody's laughing at us."

"They're not. They're taking no notice."

"Yeah. The lads don't even talk to us now. They think it's stupid. That's why they stay away."

They stood at the cross near the school. Jenny Wrottle, lollipop stick raised, waited for them. Sheree turned coaxingly to Kimbo.

"Give it a last go, eh?"

That was enough. Kimbo raised her voice again.

"No, I won't give it a last go. I'm sick and tired. It's breaking our gang up, and if you want to mess about with it, I don't."

With that she ran across the road, leaving Sheree and Kimbo staring.

"Oh dear. Soon met, soon parted," said Jenny Wrottle shaking her head.

Next day, Gail and Sheree walked to school on their own. Kimbo marched along the other pavement. They looked at one another and made a face.

"Well, it's just us two now," said Sheree.

Chapter 3

THAT NIGHT GAIL went to Aunt
Mandy's in a thoughtful mood. She'd
started this search for the Greenies as a
bit of a lark. Now it was turning
serious. Kimbo and Sheree had always
been special friends. Gail had been odd
one out. Now it looked as though she
was getting between them. And Kimbo
even accused her of breaking up the
six.

She had to get something to happen
to make it worthwhile. Sheree had

49

gone along so far. And she wouldn't let sulky Kimbo push her around. But after the row Sheree was more doubtful.

"Do you think all this trouble means we shouldn't be doing this, Gail?" she asked.

"Don't see why?" said Gail defiantly. "Look, let's give it one more go."

She spent an hour at Aunt Mandy's searching through the yellowed pages of the old book. Then, almost at the end she found something that made her jump up.

"Aunt Mandy." She rushed into the kitchen, waving the book. "Can I have a lend of this?"

Aunt Mandy slowly shook her head.

"Sorry, Gail love. It's a bit rare for lending." She paused and looked

shrewdly at Gail. "I'm not sure you
should get too involved in things like
that."

Gail made a face and went
reluctantly back into the front room.
Then, as she stood in front of the
bookshelf, she had a sudden surge of
irritation with Aunt Mandy. She
looked quickly, guiltily towards the
kitchen, then slipping the book into her
bag, she called loudly, " 'Bye, Aunt
Mandy," and slipped out of the house.

Next dinner time she showed Sheree the page she had discovered.

"We got it all wrong, see. Those other things we did are to protect you from harm if you see or hear the Greenies. This is how you get them to come. This is the real thing."

Her excitement made Sheree's doubts vanish.

"OK, what do we need?"

Gail held up the battered brown book and read slowly.

"Sallet oil."

"What's that?"

"Oh, mayonnaise or olive oil," guessed Gail.

"What else?"

"Rose water."

"Oh, I can get some of that. I can borrow a bit from the bottle on my sister's dressing table," said Sheree.

"Marigold flower."

"Oh blow. They're not out yet."

"What about marsh marigolds on the pond? We can get a bud and open it."

"Oh, that's near enough. Hey, this is great."

"Hollyhock buds, wild thyme, young hazel leaves . . ."

"Where'll we get them?"

They stared at each other. Then both said, "Jenny Wrottle."

That afternoon, they knocked on the cottage door near to the school where Jenny lived with her ancient dad. Jenny looked out at them carefully, blue eyes sharp in her lined, sunburnt face.

"What for?"

Gail shuffled her feet.

"Just for something we're trying."

Jenny went back through the cottage into the garden. Gail and Sheree looked at one another, excited. Jenny returned with a paper bag.

"Now, you watch out what you're up to. And *don't* eat or drink anything."

What she meant they couldn't guess, but they turned and ran in silent excitement.

Chapter 4

FOR THREE DAYS the jar, holding the ingredients, stood on the bank hidden among the oak roots, but where the sun could warm it. And they were lucky. Every day the sun shone. Every day the air grew warmer, heavier. Every day Gail and Sheree walked to school together. They had given up trying to say hello to Kimbo. The lads left them to it. If Sheree had doubts she hid them, while Gail grew more tense by the day.

She sneaked the old book back on to the shelf at Aunt Mandy's. Her aunt gave her a strange look.

"You're not up to something, are you Gail, love?"

"Oh no," answered Gail lightly and ran out of the house again.

On the third day, the sun came up brightly, but clouds began to gather. First grey, then purple, they mounted across the sky till by lunch time the sun had vanished. The air was close and stifling. Everyone felt uneasy, bad-tempered.

As noon came nearer, Sheree whispered, "I'm not sure I really want to, Gail."

"You promised," Gail was fierce.

Sheree said nothing and when the bell went she followed Gail to the grass bank. Now storm clouds seemed to hang over the trees. The sky darkened. There was a chill breeze. Gail shivered.

"Ready?"

Sheree nodded, looked around. Noise from the playground seemed far away. Gail raised the jar. The liquid had turned browney-green. That didn't seem right. It should be clear like crystal. And it smelt foul. She held it out then; determinedly she poured the liquid on the soil between the oak roots.

From above came a clap of thunder. A jagged flash of lightning split the clouds. Sheree jumped and grabbed Gail's arm. The jar dropped, rolled away. Sheree struggled up to go but Gail held her.

"Wait, look and listen. We may see and not hear or hear and not see."

Both froze. The playground seemed silent now. Gail concentrated until she felt dizzy. Sheree's dark eyes were big and round.

"Wait. Wait."

"You're hurting my arm, Gail."

Gail let go.

"Sorry, Sheree. But shh. It'll soon be time to wish."

Another clap of thunder made their heads ring, then the heavens opened. Gail felt the heavy drops strike her head and shoulders. Her jacket, inside out, was going to be soaked. Sheree was on her feet.

"We'll be drenched. Oh, I wish we hadn't started this."

"Sheree," Gail cried. "That's a wish gone."

"Can't you see Gail, it isn't working."

60

"Stop whingeing. Greenies hate grumblers."

Gail seized on this thought. "They'll never come now."

"Oh you and your flaming Greenies!" Sheree took a deep breath as she glared at Gail through the curtain of rain, drops glinting on her face.

"I wish I hadn't quarrelled with Kimbo," she said in a heartfelt outburst.

"I wish you'd shut up," shouted Gail, above the thunder. Then she stopped. The third wish had gone.

Sheree got up and ran away from the bank and down across the school yard. Gail knelt alone at the foot of the oak, rain soaking through her jacket, streaming down her neck. Her hair hung over her eyes. She could barely see trees or grass. Misery filled her. She was light-headed from hunger.

Then, from a distance, marvelling, she heard a distant chuckling, giggling. A voice whispered, "Ga-il, Ga-il."

She jerked up, looked wildly about her. The rain had died down. Just below the bank on the puddled playground stood Kimbo and Sheree, arm in arm.

"Gail, Miss says you're to come in. The bell's long gone."

Gail rose. She stepped down from the bank. They took an arm each and all three raced down the slope into Class Four.

Everyone stared.

Miss gave her a telling off – but not a bad one.

Boxer gave her a towel out of his swimming kit to dry her hair.

Grunter gave her a grubby piece of meat pie from his pocket.

Gareth gave her a smile and looked out of the window.

"Hey, look at that," he called.

Miss frowned but everyone crowded round to see.

Outside the sky had half cleared. From beyond the bank, arching through the sunlight and clouds, rose a fantastic double rainbow.

"Magic," said Gareth.

Magic, thought Gail.

Gareth's Mermaid

Chapter 1

THERE WERE THREE women in Gareth's
life – his mum, Miss, and the
mermaid. Mum and Miss were public.
The mermaid was very private.

Mum was very important to Gareth.
They had moved over from Wales a
year ago, and both of them missed it.
Now Wales wasn't that far away, just a
few miles down the road, if you followed
Hob Lane far enough. That is, it used
to be before they built the by-pass right
across the lane and cut it off.

64

Now if you wanted to see the hills in the distance you would have to climb the by-pass embankment just beyond the wood behind Hob Lane School.

Just how important Mum was, everyone found out the day Gareth came to school. Gareth was small, with a pale, pointed face, and deep brown eyes. Gail noticed how long his eyelashes were, and dark like his black hair.

Someone, maybe it was Boxer, called him 'Gary', just to be friendly.

Gareth looked up at Boxer, who was nearly twice as big as him and said, "It isn't Gary, it's Gareth."

Kimbo and Sheree exchanged quick smiles, but not before Gareth saw them. He was very quick on the uptake. He looked at them all now, very seriously.

"My mum doesn't like me being called Gary."

This set Grunter off. He put a prissy smile on his broad red face, squeezed up his big lips and said, mincingly, "My mummy's vewy po . . . oooooffff!"

He didn't mean to end the sentence like that. But Gareth's head, travelling at high speed, hit him in the stomach and all the breath went out of him. He had to sit down and recover, while everyone else fell about laughing.

66

So, after that he was called Gareth and nothing else and his mum's opinions were listened to with great respect.

In fact Gareth settled in and became one of the six along with Gail, Sheree, Kimbo, Boxer and Grunter.

But people soon began to find out they had to be careful what they said about Miss, in Gareth's hearing, because Gareth adopted her too.

Miss looked a bit like Gareth's mum, round-faced, dark-haired, though she was tall while Gareth's mum was small. And while his mum walked slowly with a limp, Miss always strode everywhere quickly.

But Miss was Gareth's heroine for a special reason. Gareth was really afraid of only one thing in life – water. He hated going to the baths and wouldn't have gone at all if it weren't for Miss.

One day at the baths, Gareth was sitting by the side, at the shallow end of course, near the paddling pool and the artificial rocks, trying to make up his mind whether to go in the water or not.

Some clown from Town Road Junior – Hob Lane's big rival – came

sneaking by and pushed him in. He fell
very awkwardly, as you do when you
don't mean to dive, and landed on his
back, kicking and lashing out wildly
with his arms. He was only a few
inches below the surface but it felt as
though he'd never come up again.
Someone helped him out, choking and
gasping.

Miss who had seen it all moved
like lightning and clouted the boy
who'd shoved Gareth in. There was a
big row afterwards. Some people
reckoned she had no business to do
that; it was 'unprofessional'. But
Class Four awarded her a medal and
Gareth awarded her his life-long
devotion.

But, even to please Miss he couldn't
get used to going into the water. And
certainly not away from the shallow

end. He would do a dog paddle,
keeping his big toe on the bottom if he
thought he would sink. He couldn't get
rid of the notion that he might go
down and never come up again.

Then the mermaid came and
changed all that.

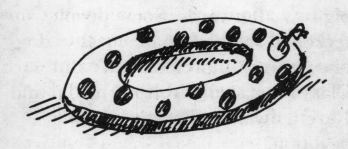

Chapter 2

MISS INTRODUCED HER, in a way. Late
one Friday afternoon she was reading
aloud for Class Four – and she read
the story about the mermaid who came
up from the Irish Sea, along the
Mersey and through an underground
cavern to emerge at certain special
times of the year in a lake not far
away. People believed if you could
catch sight of her, and speak to her,
and if she liked you, she would grant
whatever you desired.

71

In the middle of the story, Gareth, who seemed to be dreaming, burst out, "Oh, that's the same as Gwragedd Annwn."

Everyone stared. Miss put down the book.

"I beg your pardon, Gareth. Can you translate, please?"

Gareth answered, "She lived in a lake near the Black Mountain, my grannie told me. She'd come out of the

water if she was offered the right kind of bread, not doughy, not too crusty but just tasty."

Somebody started to giggle but Gareth didn't even look round. He was silent for the rest of the afternoon, thinking about the mermaid coming along the underground cavern from the sea, into the lake to grant your wishes. The thought stayed in his mind for a long time.

But he told no one, not even his mum. He kept it to himself, sometimes picturing the mermaid, just as he was going off to sleep at night. She would rise from the water, throwing back the hair from her eyes, and then look at him and smile.

"Hello, Gareth," she would say. "Are you going to swim?"

And to his own amazement, he

would stand up, raise his arms, hands together, and dive like a seal into the clear, cool water and swim, turning and twisting like a salmon.

It was only a dream. Because when he went to the baths and stood by the edge, while all around him came the echoing shouts and screams of the other children and his nostrils filled with the sharp tang of the chlorine, then his stomach would go cold and the thought of diving into that green water paralysed him.

Even Boxer, his best friend, couldn't persuade him just to jump in, holding his nose to keep the water from rushing in. He couldn't be persuaded to leave the shallow end. Often he would just stand and shiver.

Then, one day, the mermaid arrived.

Chapter 3

GARETH SAW THE mermaid sitting on
the plastic rocks by the paddling pool.
She was a little way away from him
but he could see her clearly.

Her hair was long and brown, her
eyes slanting, her arms and shoulders
white, and, sure enough, curled
beneath her was the tail, gleaming
blue, grey-pink, the scales so light they
seemed transparent.

She played with the ends of her hair
between her fingers and looked across

Paddling Pool

the water straight at him. The strange
thing was that all around her boys and
girls were scrambling, jumping,
shouting, but she took no notice and
they did not see her at all. Only
Gareth saw her and she looked only at
him. She smiled but said nothing and
then uncoiling from the rocks she
vanished into the water in a trail of
bubbles.

Gareth wanted to speak but she was
gone. She had seen him but she had
not spoken. Yet he felt she would, if
only . . .

If only. He brooded about this for
the rest of the week in the moments
before he went to sleep. But it was only
the night before the next swimming
lesson was due that he remembered the
story of the Gwragedd Annwn and the
fresh baked bread.

His mother looked at him curiously when he asked for it. But next day when Class Four went to the baths he had a slice of crisp, fresh home-baked bread in his pocket.

He had some trouble hiding it when he got into his trunks. Some people were always so nosey when you got changed. But he rolled the bread in his left hand and held it tight and hoped he would see the mermaid before he had to go in the water.

And he was in luck. She was there again. But not on the rocks at the shallow end. She was seated on the tiles halfway down where Gareth never went. The water came over his nose there. She sat, tail lazily moving to and fro in the water below and looked at Gareth. Then she smiled and moved her head as if beckoning him.

Gareth sidled away from the class. Miss was talking to them and the others did not notice him sneaking away. Now he stood opposite the mermaid. She smiled again and Gareth opened his hand to show the bread. He spoke, not aloud, but inside his head. He knew she listened.

"I've brought you some new baked bread, Lady."

"Thank you, Gareth." She did not speak aloud either, but he heard her voice in his head.

"What do you wish of me?" she asked. Her voice had a chuckle in it, but she was not teasing.

"I want to dive and swim." The words burst out silently in his head.

"But you can swim, Gareth. Everything that lives can swim. Every

living thing came from the water long
ago. Only some of us have stayed."

"I can't. I'll sink. I'll never come up
again, I know."

"You will not. The water will push
you up. Just try and get down to the
bottom. It is not as easy as you think."

Still he hesitated.

"Gareth. You will not sink. The
whale is a thousand times heavier than
you and the water holds up the
whale."

"But I don't like water," he
protested.

"The cat does not like water. But
the cat can swim, if it needs. Tigers
swim, Gareth. Be a tiger. You have the
temper."

He stood on the edge. She smiled.
He raised his arms, hands together and
braced his knees. But his feet were

rooted to the tiles. They would not
move.

Then the mermaid took a ring from
her finger and began to play with it.
The ring spun and glinted silver in the
air. It slipped and fell into the water.
She gasped, then looked coaxingly at
him.

"Gareth, Gareth, I have lost my
silver ring. Be kind and fetch it for
me."

"Gareth!"

He heard someone call from along the edge of the pool. The sound made him act. His feet freed themselves from the tiles, the air rushed past him and the water cut at shoulders, arms, stomach, stinging him.

Then he was in another world, green and darker, though above him there was light. Below him, dimly he could see the lines that marked the distances and depths. And in the middle of a black line, a small circle of silver glinted.

He struggled towards it, but the water pressed him back trying to force him to the top again. All of a sudden he remembered his swimming strokes. His arms lunged forward and downward and his feet lashed out behind him. Once, twice, then knuckles, elbows, knees all jarred on the bottom.

The water pulled at him, his lungs were bursting. He clenched his teeth as if to keep the air in, felt the metal ring between his fingers and grasping it, he let himself be snatched away, legs and arms flying, up to the top.

Hands grappled at him. Boxer was beside him in the water. Faces looked down on him from the side. They were calling his name in amazement.

Boxer pulled him to the side. Gail and Grunter leaned down and heaved him out of the water. For a second or two he crouched there on the wet tiles, dazed.

He looked down at his hands. The bread was gone. But between his fingers, the silver circle gleamed.

"Hey, Gareth. What were you up to,

man? Diving in like that. We didn't believe it."

"Yeah, fantastic dive. Why did you do it?"

Gareth held up the shining circle between his fingers to answer the questions.

"That's a ring pull, an old ring pull. You went down after that?"

"Hey, and brought it up too."

Everyone seemed amazed.

Gareth pulled the thin metal circle on to his finger and closed his hand round it. He grinned at the others. No good trying to explain to them that this was the mermaid's silver ring.

He looked along towards the rocks by the paddling pool. The mermaid was not there any more. She had gone back down the underground cavern to the sea.

But she had granted his wish. And he knew that from now on, when he dived and swam, she would not be far away.

Adventures of ZOT the DOG

Ivan Jones

Life is fun with Zot!

Zot is a lovable little dog, and he and his
friend Clive have all sorts of funny
adventures. There's the cheeky mouse
who plays tricks on them, a cunning
snake who steals all the food, and an
unhappy frog who does NOT like being
swallowed up by Zot the dog!

Also in Young Puffin

THE LITTLE EXPLORER

Margaret Joy

Join Stanley on his thrilling voyage!

The little explorer is setting out on a long
journey. He is going in search of the
pinkafrillia, the rarest flower in the
world. Together with Knots, the sailor,
and Peckish, the parrot, Stanley travels
through the jungle of Allegria. And what
adventures they all have!